Releasing the Shackles

Surviving Abuse

Danielle M. Gilbert, *Visionary Author*

Co Authored By:

Kai Banks, Alesia Bassett, Carmen Clack, Tondra Deveral, Leslie Greene, Skyy Harrison, LaKesha Monroe, Jameka Smith

Copyright © 2022 by Danielle M. Gilbert.
All Rights Reserved. This book, nor any portion thereof, may be reproduced or used in any manner whatsoever without the expressed written permission of the author(s) except for the use of brief quotations in a book review.

Printed in the United States of America.

ISBN: 979-8-9876649-0-2
Edited, Formatted and Published by Empower Her Publishing, LLC
empowerherpublishing.com

Table of Contents

Foreword..v

Love Lost by Kai Banks........................1

The Demon Within by Alesia Bassett.....9

They Call it a Fairy Tale
by Carmen Clack.............................17

Up She Rises by Tondra Devarel.........27

It's Only a Chapter by Leslie Greene.....39

Broken Pieces by Skyy Harrison...........53

The Raw Truth or a Dirty Lie
by LaKesha Monroe..........................67

Stay Woke by Jameka Smith...............77

Conclusion..................................91

Foreword
Danielle M. Gilbert

I Got My Flowers Today:

I got flowers today! It wasn't my birthday or any other special day. We had our first argument last night; And he said a lot of cruel things that really hurt; I know that he is sorry and didn't mean to say the things he said, Because he sent me flowers today.

I got flowers today. It wasn't our anniversary or any other special day. Last night, he threw me into a wall and started to choke me. It seemed like a nightmare. I couldn't believe that it was real. I woke up this morning sore and bruised all over. I know he must be sorry. Because he sent me flowers today.

I got flowers today! And it wasn't Valentine's Day or any other special day; Last night he beat me and threatened to kill me; Make-up and long sleeves didn't hide the cuts and bruises this time; I couldn't go to work today because I didn't want anyone to know—but I know he's sorry; Because he sent me flowers today.

I got flowers today! And it wasn't Mother's Day or any other special day; Last night he beat me again, and it was worse than all of the other times; If I leave him, what will I do? How will I take care of the kids? What about money? I'm afraid of him, but I'm too scared and dependent to leave him! But he must be sorry; Because he sent me flowers today.

I got flowers today. Today was a special day—it was the day of my funeral; Last night he killed me; If only I would have gathered the courage and strength to leave him; I could have received help from the Women's Shelter, but I didn't ask for their help; So I got flowers today—for the last time.

Author: Paulette Kelly

Imagine expecting to receive beautiful red and white flowers from the person who you thought loved you, cared about you or simply worshiped the ground you walked on; then to only learn that person is giving you your flowers in the form of a black eye, leaving you with no money in your account, being manipulative or emotionally draining. You may wonder what is happening. Is this real? Is something wrong with me? What did I do to this person? The answers come in many different forms.

Abuse is the unacceptable behavior of an adult or child to accomplish unwarranted or

Foreword

unsuitable reasons. Abuse can coexist with abandonment, which is defined as the inability to meet the basic physical and medical needs of a dependent person; also as emotional deficiency, and neglect. Neglect is sometimes described as passive abuse.

There are several types of abuse that individuals may experience for different reasons. The abuse shows up as:

1. Physical abuse
2. Verbal abuse
3. Emotional abuse
4. Psychological abuse
5. Sexual abuse
6. Financial abuse
7. Digital abuse/Cyberbullying
8. Workplace violence or organizational/institutional abuse

Regardless of how abuse shows up, there are many reasons why abuse occurs and why individuals stay in abusive relationships. It is not always easy for the victims of an abusive relationship to escape so simply. There are various reasons they remain in the relationship such as being under a threat, feeling worthless, believing the abuse is the norm or because of embarrassment or shame. Individuals may abuse other people for various motives, including substance use and mental health disorders. Vicious people may have suffered abuse themselves. The sequence of abuse is when kids are taught violent behaviors from being mistreated or observing abuse. The Centers for Disease Control-Child Abuse and Neglect Prevention states, "children of families with lower socioeconomic status are five times more likely to be abused or neglected, which may be partially related to increased levels of stress." Regardless of the reason, abuse is never acceptable, and it is never the fault of the victim.

The revelation about the abuse leads to shocking statistics that child abuse or neglect impacts one in seven children in the United States per year according to the Centers for Disease Control-Child Abuse and Neglect Prevention. Similarly, The National Coalition Against Domestic Violence has estimated that one in four women and one in seven men in the United States have been injured by an intimate partner. Unfortunately, many who experience the abuse feel that they need to survive and avoid taking the risk of a bad ending, so they feel threatened and remain. The victim(s) often feel love for their perpetrator, may have children with them, hope the abuser will change by stopping the abusive

Foreword

behavior or are simply blind by the abuser's behavior that they do not realize their relationship is unhealthy.

The impacts of abuse are physical, emotional, and psychological harm and sometimes even death. There has also been a link between abuse including financial, emotional, and psychological abuse and suicide. Many victims being abused develop PTSD (post-traumatic stress disorder), depression and anxiety. Sexual abuse can lead to unwanted pregnancy, sexually transmitted diseases, and depression. In addition, abuse can lead to trauma where the victims become emotionally attached to their abusers and go through imbalance of power in relationships and continuous harm.

Subsequently, I remember receiving my flowers in many different forms such as physical, verbal, emotional, and psychological abuse. Pain. Heartache. Frustration. Confusion. Loneliness. These emotions flowed through my body every second, minute and hour of the day for years. Why did the man I loved harm my first-born child? The only other person I felt loved me, smiled and was happy just to cuddle in my arms. Michael Leon Ross entered eternal life on September 26, 1997. I thought the emotional abuse would never end.

Danielle M. Gilbert

Oh, how I was so wrong. The abuse continued with the word no family wants to hear: cancer. The family learned my mother had leukemia. As a young child, I was confused about what cancer meant and how it could harm my precious mother. I continued with my life of going to school and hanging with my girlfriends. The thought of my mother not making it through the pain never crossed my mind. She was a fighter - one who knew how to survive every obstacle that came her way.

The morning of May 28, 1998, the phone rang. "Hello, may I speak to Mr. Ross?" "Sure, hold please." Awkward silence entered the room. Minutes later, the words I never wanted to hear, "Your mother did not make it. She did not make it out of the coma." No way. Not my mother. Pain. Heartache. These are the emotions that streamed through every bone in my body. The abuse felt like a knife of devastation through the center of my heart. I fell to the floor in tears - confused and lost, asking why.

Six months later, the pain heightened as my uncle, aunt and grandfather entered eternal life. Nightly, I fell to my knees, hands together, praying to my Heavenly Father to remove the pain of abuse from my life. Although I prayed to remove the abuse, the physical and verbal abuse

Foreword

showed up in relationships. All of these forms of abuse led to imbalance in my career, friendships, relationships and how I showed up for myself. Whew, patience. I never understood how to be patient with life - most importantly, with God's plan for me.

Some days it was a lot harder to be patient. Day after day I prayed with no response. I asked why my prayers were falling on deaf ears. Why won't God move me into a place of happiness? Sitting on the edge of my bed on a Sunday afternoon, I prayed for the Spirit to fill me, empower me and direct me as I waited on the Lord. I must admit, the silence was slowly killing me inside. The silence led to depression and anxiety. For years, I was trying to find ways to cope and deal with the abuse. Beyond taking medication and talking to a therapist, I needed to find a way to improve my overall well-being and quality of life after the abuse. Therefore, it was important to prioritize both my mental and physical health through quality sleep, managing stress, and learning how to care for myself. In addition, it was also important to be aware of thoughts and work on developing healthy self-talk. This is a skill that was learned and practiced with a trained psychologist or psychiatrist. Through the pain of death, learning myself, seeking help and praying, I never knew God was preparing me for His destiny, or rather my destiny that He designed especially for me.

If you are experiencing abuse in any form, please know that you are not alone. Through the stories of these women, I pray you find the strength and courage to seek help in order to receive your flowers while on earth. Remember, abuse is never the fault of the victim.

"You've gotta dance like there's nobody watching, love like you'll never be hurt, sing like there's nobody listening, and live like it's heaven on earth."
-William W. Purkey

Love Lost
Kai Banks

"When we understand love as the will to nurture our own and another's spiritual growth, it becomes clear that we cannot claim to love if we are hurtful and abusive." - Bell Hooks

I have learned to understand that love is not just a feeling, but an action. Love is a verb. In order to say you love someone, you must actively pour into them. We can't just say we love someone and not care for them, commit to them, acknowledge them, trust them, feel a sense of responsibility for them, respect them, and work to understand them.

"This experience of genuine love (a combination of care, commitment, trust, knowledge, responsibility, and respect)..." - Bell Hooks

Bell Hooks, and my own experience, has taught me love isn't just the feeling of butterflies or happiness. Sometimes love looks like saying no if it means that the person you love will be better off or even you might be better off. At times, love can be one-sided; but ultimately, it should be mutual. Bell Hooks said love and abuse cannot coexist. Similarly, light and darkness cannot coexist.

I choose love and light.

Sitting at the bottom of the staircase in the dark, I could make out his silhouette hanging over me like a dark cloud. I stayed there hoping he would calm down, praying for health and safety over my unborn son. I thought, *how the hell did I get here?*

I was 18 and in my first year of college when I found out that I was pregnant by Lost. This was not what I had envisioned for my future when I packed up my room and left Richmond to attend Old Dominion University in Norfolk, VA. As I waved goodbye to my family from inside of my dorm, I remember being excited to begin the pursuit of happiness, independence, and freedom. Ever since I was a little girl I had dreamed of working in litigation or social work. My plan was to graduate college, travel, and create a successful career. Instead, I found myself pregnant, on academic probation and "in Love" with a man I barely knew. How the fuck did I end up the statistic? My very own case study. The eldest daughter who was most likely to succeed had become a young mom, a victim of domestic abuse, and was on the verge of getting kicked out of school.

Love Lost

I didn't fall in love with an abuser. I fell in love with a charming, handsome, intelligent man. He took me out on dates and made me feel special. I enjoyed spending time with his family and touring his hometown, Baltimore, MD. We had fun together. Love bombing was my first red flag and I didn't even recognize it because it looked like what I thought was Love. Love bombing is described as the practice of showing a person excessive affection and attention as a way of manipulating them in a relationship.

The first time he got physical was after he became angry about a decision that I made. He wasn't wrong to be angry, but he was wrong to put his hands on me. I didn't recognize it as a red flag. I was young and thought it was natural to be a little jealous and lose control of one's emotions. He pushed me but he didn't mean to. I didn't think it would happen again. But the abuse continued and the cycle began. I wanted to leave but I felt stuck spinning in this wheel of highs and lows. Sometimes life would be great, other times it felt like torture. The more reality set in that I was going to become a mother, I redirected my dark thoughts into positive thoughts and mustered up enough strength to work part-time and complete my third semester. I gave birth to my son at the end of that semester. . He became my "why" and I strived to love him the way that I was taught to love.

I put forth my best effort to create a safe and loving environment for my son. I poured every bit of what I could into him and his father. I became a wife and focused on surviving and coming out of it rather than acknowledging what was happening. I endured the abuse thinking it was best to keep the family together. I made excuses and denied that it was even happening. At times I even blamed myself. I didn't realize the impact that trauma has on the brain, but it is very real. The mind is the most powerful organ in your body and the most fragile. The abuse became routine and normal. Some years would be better than others. After a while it became surreal, as if I had entered an alternate universe and when it was over, I was back home.

For years, I knew I needed to leave, wanted to leave, and even tried to leave. The first time I left was on the auto train from Orlando, FL to Lorton, VA for over 12 hours with a son to the left of me and another in my stomach. I was determined to protect and provide for my boys. My mother had purchased my ticket and it was her love for me that brought me out of the darkness. She sent me positive affirmations, checked on me, and was committed to my health and well-being. Although she didn't agree with many of my decisions, she never stopped respecting me, trusting me, or believing in me.

She continues to push me and even take care of me. She embraced me every single time I came back home and even required me to go to counseling to pursue a journey of healing and spiritual growth. Others poured into me in increments but my Mother's Love was like no other.

When I made the decision to leave my abusive marriage for good, I really didn't know what to expect. In my mind, I had failed yet again. I grew up with both my mother and father and wanted to provide a familiar structure for my sons. My ultimate goal was to give them everything I had. I learned that love wasn't just the fuzzy feeling in your stomach, long nights on the phone, or getting married. Love is actionable. It took me a long time, and a lot of heartbreak, to learn what love is and I believe it will take a lifetime to master it. For now, I will continue to practice the act of loving.

We all have endured abuse from family members who "love" us. Most times we experience abuse through oppression, gaslighting, and/or narcissism in our very own society. The systems we are connected to abuse us financially, emotionally, and even physically. We receive messaging that love is about sex, marriage, or a fairy tale. I understand how love can be misunderstood. I got married thinking that because we "loved" each other, we would be able to make it work - if not for us, at least for our sons. I joined the church and went to counseling but none of those things worked. I was young and hadn't learned to love myself. As I matured, I began educating myself and evolving. I started to understand how abuse impacts the body and began to see the effects clearly.

Being in an abusive relationship changed me forever. There are parts of me that I don't recognize from before. The painful moments I do remember are etched in my brain like a tattoo. I have a scar on the right side of my forehead and the left side of my lips. Some moments have faded, others have become permanent and real. But the good thing about being in your darkest hour is you aren't afraid anymore when the lights go out. Overcoming abuse made me stronger and desire to love better. I attended group counseling sessions. I volunteered in my community. I became active and practiced loving myself. I developed a five-year plan, wrote it down, and began working towards it. I went back to school, fixed my credit, bought a house, and worked in the career field that I dreamed of as that freshman in college. Within 10 years, every goal from that five-year plan was accomplished.

Love Lost

It has been over a decade since leaving my abusive relationship. For years, I tried to hold my abuser accountable for his actions, cursing him every time I ran into an obstacle knowing that if I just or if he hadn't. On the day he apologized and asked for my forgiveness, I felt a sense of relief. But on the day that I truly forgave him, I released it all. It by far has not been easy, but it has been worth it. I choose love.

Kai Banks is a passionate, positive, and fierce woman. She is a servant leader, solutions-oriented, and resourceful. She is an overcomer of domestic violence, a mother of three boys, and a community advocate. Her professional career consists of developing young adults as they transition into adulthood to become more engaged community members. Her personal endeavors include facilitating conversations around community issues. She has been featured in the Richmond Times-Dispatch, Richmond Magazine, Richmond Free Press, Style Weekly, and the documentary, This is Black. She is a proud AmeriCorps Alumni and advocate for Richmond Public Schools. She has obtained an Associates of Arts degree at the Community College

Kai Banks

of Baltimore County and is currently pursuing a Bachelors at Virginia Commonwealth University in Political Science and Nonprofit Management. She enjoys watching professional football and dancing to live music. Kai strives to live an extraordinary life by living fearlessly, exploring new ventures, and partnering with the community to create solutions for residents in the city of Richmond.

The Demon Within
Alesia Bassett

Remember "there is no fear in love" (1 John 4:18).

The day comes when you meet a person who is perfect for you. So, you thought. He is charming, attentive and giving. His smile just draws you in. Then comes the day you meet the demon within.

It started out a good day. A guy I was dating and I attended a networking event with wine tasting. There was a guest speaker from my hometown. We continued to socialize and everything seemed fine. After getting home, he expressed he had an issue with me paying attention to the speaker. In his mind, I wanted this man. I did not take him seriously because it sounded like a joke to me. I was getting ready to take a shower when he walked into the bathroom, grabbed me from behind and threw me to the floor. He repeatedly hit me while ranting like a madman about being disrespected. I made my way out the bathroom and into the bedroom. He grabbed me again and dragged me back to the bathroom and started filling the tub up with water. He tried to put my head under the water in the tub but I fought, kicked and screamed. He finally gave up after I kept saying, "What are you doing? This is not you." When someone shows you who they are, believe them. I sat on the floor near my bed and tried to make sense of what had just happened. It seemed unreal. The look in his eyes while he was in a rage was one of the scariest things I have ever seen. I think back and ask myself, "why did I not put him out at that time?" If I am being honest with myself, I was thinking this would be a one-time occurrence. *I'm a loyal, honest, loving person that was misunderstood. He will see that I am not disrespectful.* I thought these things to myself and believed he would see the real me and never hurt me again. I told no one about what happened.

From that point on, there were many other incidents that cannot be explained.

*He would call me at work and want to stay on the phone the entire time I'm working.

*He accused me of watching the back of a bald-headed man's head at the movie theater.

*I was accused of watching a young boy at my company picnic.

*I was accused of paying attention to a man at the gas station.

*He accused me of sitting in a position so that his family could see under my dress.

*I was told to walk with my eyes facing the ground when we were together.

Of course, the physical abuse was not a one-time occurrence and began again. It was at that time I started to document with words, recordings and pictures. However, it was New Year's Day 2019 when my documentation backfired. He woke me up by grabbing my hair and dragging me across the living room floor. "I'm not going to jail for anyone," he said. He had found the notes I had been recording in my phone. He beat me in the head so no one could see the bruises. I had all the signs of a concussion. After that incident, I kept my documentation in my office at work.

Sadly, I could not figure out his triggers. He only drank socially and did not do drugs. Ironically, when he drank, that was when he was on his best behavior. He told me about his abandonment issues. His mom left him with his grandmother and he did not know who his father was. We females think we can fill a void and fix whatever a man is lacking by being loving, caring and supportive. That is not the case.

As females we hope, help and heal.

We hope the behavior will change. We hope the relationship will survive.

We want to help him become a better person. We want to help him realize he is better than what he is presenting to us.

We want to heal whatever he experienced in the past. We want to heal him with unconditional love.

We do this without consideration for our own well-being.

I've played my situation over and over in my head. How could I let this happen to me? Why did this happen to me? Understand there is no certain type of female this happens to. Education does not matter. Economic status does not matter. Skin color does not matter. Physical attributes do not matter. Good character does not matter. It is NOT our fault. Leave the "if I would have", "if I could have" or "I should have" behind. The sooner we come to terms with that, the sooner we can start our personal healing journey.

It was almost three years into the relationship when I got completely out. I felt I had to be strategic with my moves. The crazy part is, the documenting had started because I needed to put it in writing to remind me this was really happening. I believed he was capable of causing severe harm. I did not want him to get away with it because I had not told anyone. Once he was actually out of the apartment, I had the locks changed. I sold my car and purchased a car he would not recognize. He was coming to my job and apartment to see if my car was there. He was stalking me. When he would come to the apartment, he would beg to come in and I would not let him. That is when he would become irate. He threatened to kill me at one point and that's when I told my oldest daughter who lived in another state. Every day while driving home, she stayed on the phone with me until I got into my apartment and searched every room. My daughter knew to send the police if something happened while we were on the phone or if she did not hear from me.

I printed several copies of every written word I had documented up to that point. I made sure to put his full name and I gave a copy to my sister, my daughters, my friend and a co-worker. I told them if anything happened to me, he did it. These documents detailed incidents like a phone conversation he and I had had where he told me how he would carefully plan to kill someone, down to details like how long he would plan before the killing, his alibi, location and more. The documentation also included a time when he called me after we were no longer together and said "you're dead, bitch" and hung up. He then called right back and said, "watch your back" before hanging up again. Later that day he called again speculating about me being in a new relationship, although there was no one new in my life. He told me to tell the man to enjoy me while he could, because it wouldn't last. He said "payback is a bitch and he is going to be that bitch." He told me how he started to come to my apartment the night before and put a gun to my head. He was waiting at my apartment and wanted me to come there right now. I refused, hung up the phone and called one of his relatives. She told me he had called their house the night before asking to borrow a gun.

I was consumed with fear and anger for a period of time. How dare he live like nothing ever happened? When I finally came to terms to let go and let GOD, his life started to change. In October 2022, a detective came to my job wanting to know if I knew of his whereabouts. I had not had contact with him. Imagine my surprise when they told me the last place they tracked him was in my new city and state in September 2022. Apparently, he is on the run for some recent warrants in Chesterfield County, VA.

I pray. I pray. I pray.

Alesia Sorina Bassett grew up in New Orleans, LA and is the oldest of four siblings. She married at the age of 18, raised a family of four and stayed married for over 32 years. Alesia received a BA from Loyola University in Human and Organizational Development at the age of 40. After weathering KATRINA, she relocated to Virginia only to return to Louisiana 15 years later to face Covid-19 that took the life of her oldest daughter. She is a fan of live music and dance.

They Call it a Fairy Tale
Carmen Clack

I was recently told that my life story is a fairytale and I thought about that for days. I am under the leadership of Community Christian Center's Pastor Julius White where he states that "if you misdefine, you will misassign." That thought process led me to think about what a fairytale means so I looked up its definition. Here is what I found: 1. something resembling a fairy tale in being magical, idealized, or extremely happy. 2. a fabricated story, especially one intended to deceive. As of today, I am 45 years old, happily married, and the mother of four. I'm still a work in progress but now I understand what love is and what it means to me - not only how to love but the kind of love I want to receive as well. My picture may not be perfect, but I can honestly say that I am blessed to have the life I have today. This is not my story, but His grace, and that means there is nothing I did to deserve it, but He always covered me and kept me safe. Now let me tell you how I survived abuse…

Let's think about this word "abuse" and let me dissect how and why I accepted it for so long. My thoughts, opinions, perception, mentality, and emotions as related to love were learned from what I endured and saw as a child. So, abuse found me through my own misguided misconceptions of what love was. Fast forward to high school, I was 16 years old, pregnant, and soon to be a single mom because the father decided he did not want to be a dad. I then met a guy who presented himself as if he wanted to give me the world, which soon turned into control which made me doubt myself. He wanted me to look a certain way so he would buy my clothes. He wanted me to act a certain way so he would teach me who I needed to be. I would hear this little voice in my head that would tell me this is not who or what I needed in my life. I cannot recall exactly what led to me getting out of the relationship, but I can recall having this intense feeling of knowing it was over for me, so I finally walked away.

By 17 years old, I was living life as a single parent. I also had to deal with the loss of my father, the only person I had to protect me. Of course, life happened in between, but by the time I was in my early twenties, I realized just how much of me was still broken from what I never healed from. I had begun working and living each day taking care of my son. I was just trying to create a better life and figure out what was next for us. Then here comes this man, eight years older than me, who presented himself as a well-rounded man who could teach me some things about life. He represented that "better life" I had imagined for my son and myself. I soon found out that he was a nightmare, not a dream, so this was no fairytale. His abuse and control began so subtly at first. For a while, I couldn't tell that he was trying to gain control of my mind through his manipulations that were disguised as love. Those subtle queues were evident in the way he wanted to isolate me from my friends and family, needing to know my whereabouts and having to do constant check-ins. Not to mention, my free time was his; I had no say in how the time would be spent. His behavior triggered that little voice again that started to tell me that this was not love, so I began to push back with his requests. I denied him full control of my life and this led to those once subtle queues becoming obvious signs of abuse.

Carmen Clack

He was a completely different person around people than who I experienced when we were alone. He could be charming, a good listener, a good friend, and a good guy, but no one knew the monster I endured behind closed doors. For instance, there was a time when he put a gun to my head while my son watched and threatened to kill the both of us. I can also remember the time he was choking me so long that the blood vessels in my face started to pop and I almost passed out. In my mind, I had nowhere to go and nobody to turn to because he had done what he intended to do: isolated me and convinced me that he was all I had. This place once considered home had turned into hell and I was now pregnant with my second child. That little voice was back again telling me to leave. This was not love.

Although fearful, that physical harm to me gave me the strength to leave, especially because I had a life growing inside of me. However, those broken places inside of me were still unhealed because when he showed up with his charm to convince me he would be better, I believed him and went back. Now he knew I would leave so the gifts and the facade of this wonderful life got better for all to see. Meanwhile, the abuse towards me got worse. Behind closed doors, I was living in such a nightmare. Each day would be a mystery because I did not know if abuse was coming. Would I be accused and abused because he had to have a "reason" to put his hands on me? There were cameras in the home and recording devices on the phones just to track me. I was a prisoner in my own life, not just my home. The pain attached to this abuse was embedded in mind control. I can see that clearly now because even with hospital visits, black eyes, and broken bones, I would make excuses for him. I had this sense of loyalty to him, this love for him, which overshadowed the fact that I was afraid of him. I had learned some of his triggers and tried to conform as much as possible, but even that did not save me. Sexual abuse was an added layer that I thought could not get any worse. I soon became pregnant with my third child who I gave up for adoption because my child deserved a way out, even if I did not have one. That pregnancy shifted my mental state and that little voice that never really left me was telling me this is not love and I needed to leave, but I had no idea how.

I stayed and tried to develop a plan because just leaving was not realistic. My life was controlled by this man and I believed he loved me. Every level of this abuse continued and in less than two years, I ended up pregnant again with my fourth child. I gave this child up for adoption as well because I was still living in hell and this hell had no place for another child. The torture and torment continued, but when the abuse took aim at my children, I made the decision to send my firstborn to live with my sister and I would soon navigate a way out for my second child and myself. My mind was wrapped in what I had come to believe about myself because of what this boy I thought was a man had convinced me to think of myself and what I thought about love. I was scared for my future, and unsure of a future, because after six years, this was the only life I had known.

I can remember it like yesterday - after he left the house on a Sunday morning, I grabbed my child and we left, never looking back. That little voice consumed me and gave me everything I needed to walk away. I have talked about that little voice this entire time because it was always there and I know that it was the Holy Spirit. His Grace never forsake me, but always covered me, even in my own fear. I did not realize that it was God ensuring I made it through. One thing I learned was that leaving was half the battle. The other half was learning how to love myself because I had to rediscover who I was and rebuild from the ground up.

I have heard it said before that another person cannot teach you how to love yourself, but my testimony contradicts that statement. Eventually, I met an amazing man who became my husband. He had a level of patience in him that allowed me to learn to love myself. His love pushed me to learn what love truly was and what love was going to mean to me and for me. There is a difference between someone wanting from you and someone wanting for you. The difference is truly being loved because my healing was a priority even while learning to be in this new relationship. I wish I could say that the signs are easy to spot for abuse; however, there is a thin line that is easier to see when you love yourself, because when you know and love yourself, then you can tell the difference between someone who is there for you versus someone who is there to use you. The most valuable thing I learned from enduring hell was that I had lost myself and needed to find her again.

If today I am living a fairytale, it is through His grace, through understanding love, through patience, through letting go, through acceptance of things I cannot change, and it is through understanding that perfection is moot. Surviving abuse is my testimony because there are so many who do not survive, who do not make it out, and who do not share their story. There are so many still in abusive situations because the picture-perfect image is what they have been programmed to believe in. Throughout my journey, a lot could be said, opinions could be formed - both negative and positive - but what's important for me is that I am free. I can heal and I can help someone else make the decision to leave. I told these fragments of my story to show that in time, wounds heal but the scars remain. I still have triggers and self-doubt. I still feel angry and wish I made different choices and wonder what if. My journey did not stop in that hell. I am the woman I am today because I endured and survived. I decided to trust in love and learn what love truly is. I also understand now more than ever that without God and His grace, I would not be here today. To reflect on my past, I can say that I have come so far from where I started: mentally, emotionally, and physically. Most importantly, my story is not over yet. I hope and pray that my story can be someone's strength to know that they can make it out of an abusive relationship too. That hold is not a chain you cannot break; trust me, you can break free. Even in the darkest times, remember that you are not alone; your faith can guide you through any storm, but you must choose yourself and have the will to trust yourself even in your uncertainty. It is not always easy to keep the faith in challenging times, but that is why you walk by faith not by sight. From hell to a fairytale, not the defined version, but the fairytale I created and deserve for me. Everything is not perfect, but well worth it. My life today is better than I could have ever imagined.

Carmen Clack is a mother, grandmother, sister, daughter, and wife. She has a huge heart for her family and is known for being a selfless person. She is passionate about serving others and uses her past experiences as fuel to carry out her

Carmen Clack

purpose of inspiring others to live a more fulfilled life. Carmen acknowledges that she has come quite a long way in her journey, but is still traveling to reach her final destination. As such, she recognizes that her assignment in this season is to build so that she can continue to grow and be better with each new day.

Up She Rises
Tondra Devarel

Champions Are Made Here - No Title Needed to Move Forward!

You are not bound by what people say, the history of your family, your finances, or your health.

Lead when commanded to lead. Minister when called to minister. Do not move ahead of faith or slower in faith, but in line with faith. His love for me keeps me laser-focused on Him and I trust Him every step of the way. Why? Because He led me to a place of righteousness even when I was judged, looked down on and talked about. Thank You, Lord, that my soul is tied to You and I say thank You for the guidance, support and redemption. I will stay rooted in the word for the word is forever living, breathing, adaptable and changing.

Tondra Devarel

We have all heard the saying, never judge a book by its cover. What exactly does that mean? Many will say that we should look to the mind and not to one's outward appearance. What about the fact that judging others makes us blind? Wow, if only I had known that back then. You see the truth is, my deliverance came when I became sick and tired of being sick and tired - mentally, physically and emotionally.

When I was a child, another child told me that I was born out of wedlock and that I was a bastard child. Having no clue what that meant, I went to my mother to tell her what the child said. She became furious but never took the time to explain to me what it meant. I then opened up the dictionary and read the meaning for myself. That is the day that changed my life and I began thinking I wasn't just a child, but an illegitimate child. I began to question why and how this happened. I started feeling like I was not whole and was embarrassed and judgmental towards my mother. I watched her date and then marry a man who almost destroyed our relationship. He never wanted her to show me any attention and he disliked me for no reason. He became abusive to her and tried to be abusive to me but I stood up for myself. I told my mom that if we had each other then he couldn't harm us. He wanted to feel like he had power and control over both my mother and me.

He didn't want us to have friends and he would sometimes walk around the house with a gun in his hand. No one really knew what went on in the home because I wasn't allowed to share this with anyone. He told my mom that if he ever went to jail that he would kill both of us. I could have left and went to stay with my dad but I knew what my mother was going through and I didn't want to leave her. Staying there did more harm than good because I would stay in my room with the door closed. When my mom and I went shopping, she would have to hide whatever she bought for me because he didn't want me to have anything. I felt that he was a man with a mean spirit and pretended to be nice in public and around family members.

I later started dating and ended up pregnant my senior year of high school. Here I was having a child out of wedlock and just getting ready to complete high school. I felt like a curse was on me and kept asking God "why me?" The answers finally came and the first one was that the Bible says "honor your mother and your father and your days will be longer here on earth." I thought to myself, I am doing just that. Yet, God allowed me to live a mirror image of my mom's life and the truth is, I had no clue that I was headed in the same direction as her and needed her for support and guidance during my ordeal.

Tondra Devarel

I was a teenage mother who had to hide my pregnancy and then have the father of my child deny that the child was his. It was an embarrassing and painful moment for me. My plans to attend college were put on hold and five years later, I was pregnant with my second child, married to my second child's father and we moved into our first home. We were unequally yoked. He loved to drink and party and I didn't. This resulted in many arguments that then led to physical abuse. I stayed in this relationship when I should have left. I felt that I would be judged by others and had read that twenty percent of marriages fail within the first five years. I wanted to not be one of the twenty percent. I wanted a family picture with both a husband and wife for my kids. I wanted the same thing that my mother wanted for me and I experienced the same pain that she experienced trying to give it to me.

Have you ever wondered what makes people stay in toxic/abusive relationships? I stayed in mine because I feared being judged. This is why it is important to have empathy and not judge other people's situations. It is a beautiful thing when we accept the fact that other people's opinions don't matter. We are not going to be liked by everyone and we are not going to like everyone. Life has a tendency of making us feel less than if we don't fall in line with the majority.

Up She Rises

The pain was real and the struggle to find peace was also real. I began to silence myself to hear the small inner voice speak. I began to pray daily for discernment. The voice said if you will take one step forward then I will take two. This is the day that changed my life. I apologized to my mother for judging her during her bad marriage. It isn't enough to acknowledge your wrong and not correct it. I had to ask for forgiveness and immediately I was set free.

Soon after, I began planning my escape from the abuse. At first I wanted to keep the home that we had built together, but God said to me "you are the one who wants out. Wanting out does come with a sacrifice. Do you not trust Me to bless you with more? Are you going to allow this home to stand in the way of you being set free?" I then asked my husband at the time if he'd be willing to refinance the home so that my name is removed and he agreed. I sought a lawyer for guidance as I wanted to be fair and reasonable and didn't want to be labeled as the bitter ex-wife. I cut off all communication with him and allowed the kids to have their relationship with him. It was important for me to heal and to build my self-confidence so that I would no longer feel victimized.

One night, I couldn't sleep and something kept telling me to check my husband's pants pockets.

Tondra Devarel

I found a receipt for a gun that he had purchased. I woke the kids up and left and waited until the next day to pack our belongings. The next day was cold and rainy, but I returned to the house, packed our things and took them to my Auntie's house where we would be staying until I found a new place to stay. He did finally return home around noon and told me that he didn't want me to go, but he knew that he couldn't make me stay. He said if I ever needed anything, he would always be there. I thought, *if you loved, respected, cared and honored me, I wouldn't be leaving. The streets got the attention that I should have been receiving and you owe me nothing. Take care of yourself. You are now free to do the things that mattered most to you.* This was one of the toughest decisions I had to make in life. It took years for me to move out of my own way and to forgive myself. I had no idea that my decision to leave my husband would be judged by so many and that I would lose some married friends along the way. I had support from my family and friends and we all did what we needed to do to get me gone.

A few weeks after moving in with my Aunt, I was at work one morning when my superiors called everyone who had the same title as me into a meeting. I was shaking. I thought we were getting ready to be laid off. Instead, they changed our title and increased our salary. For me, this salary increase was double what I was making. I went from $25,000 to $50,000. All I could do was cry because God told me that if I took one step, He would take two. I then began looking for an apartment in January and had completed an application when my best friend called and told me that there was a house that a coworker of hers was selling. She wanted to buy it but she knew that my kids and I needed it more. She wanted to give me first choice at buying it if I wanted it. I went to see the home the day before the seller was hosting an open house and immediately, God spoke and said "this is it!" The seller had tears in her eyes and she said, "I know the spirit by the spirit and I will do all that I can within reason to see that you and your kids have this home if that is your desire." The kids and I had moved out of our home a few days before Christmas in 2005 and I closed on this home on March 15, 2006. Can we say the favor of God was on me? I was reminded of Romans 12:6: God would not lead me somewhere and then leave me.

In life, we have to let God be our guide. We have all heard the saying, "He will never leave us or forsake us," but then we doubt Him when things don't go as planned. He made us in His image and He holds the key to our breakthrough. He is just waiting for us to surrender to Him. We need to turn to Him and trust Him more than we trust the voices that we hear in our heads. The voices that keep us wondering, doubting, fearing and more importantly, the voice that tells us that we can't start over again. No matter what you are facing, there is always an opportunity ahead waiting for you. If you passionately seek the Lord, you will lack nothing.

Pain is real and struggle is real but we have to understand that they are also temporary. You have to embrace positive affirmations. Affirmations remind us that we are what we think and can be used to help build our self-confidence. You do have the power to control yourself and your actions. Your words really do matter and you have the power to break every generational curse. According to The Gospel Coalition, a "generational curse describes the cumulative effect on a person of things that their ancestors did, believed, or practiced in the past, and a consequence of an ancestor's actions, beliefs, and sins being passed down." I believe that God is our guide and that there is power in the name of Jesus to break every chain. Psalm 37:23-24 says, "The Lord directs the steps of the godly. He delights in every detail of their lives. Though they stumble, they will never fall, for the Lord holds them by the hand." Proverbs 16:9 reminds us that "we can make our plans, but the Lord determines our steps." He is the giver of grace and wisdom. I challenge you to be specific about the guidance you need and learn to pray out loud. Praying out loud represents a bold move in your faith and it helps your kids know the power of praying out loud.

I love this saying by John Piper: "If you can't see the sun you will be impressed with a street light. If you've never felt thunder and lightning you'll be impressed with fireworks, and if you turn your back on the greatness and majesty of God you'll fall in love with a world of shadows and short-lived pleasures." I had to learn to love without any hidden agenda. I had to give up my expectations and learn to love someone for who they are and not for who I needed them to be. We all want to be loved, have a committed relationship and live a happy life. We can't get there if we do not acknowledge the unhappy moments.

The final truth is that I didn't want to tell this story. I was attending the final day of the Onward 2022 event at a local Marriott hotel in Richmond, VA. I was trying to take a picture but my phone opened up to Facebook and a post by Danielle Gilbert, the Visionary Author of this book, was on the screen about her call for co-authors to share their stories of surviving abuse. I immediately closed the app and all of a sudden, I felt that it was now my time. I left the event and drove to the bank. I sat at the bank still thinking about the day full of events and then I proceeded to walk towards the bank to go inside. As I was crossing the street, a car drove up and the woman inside said "hey lady." I looked and it was Danielle. It was further confirmation that it was time. I started crying because I couldn't believe that God had her come to me because He knew that I wasn't going to reach out to her. At that moment, I knew that God delivered me so that I could tell my story to save someone else.

Up She Rises is to remind us that we fall down but we can get back up again. Those who rise above the storm have one trait in common: they never give up.

Up She Rises

Tondra Devarel *is a trusted expert REALTOR®, offering 15 plus years of real estate experience in the Richmond, Virginia area. She prides herself on being your knowledgeable, professional and supportive expert REALTOR®. She has an established track record in representing the concerns of home buyers and sellers by making sure that the client's interest is the number one priority. Tondra attributes her success to the moral, intellectual, and core values that she received from her loving mother who believes that giving back and helping others, is not only a gift, but an opportunity to share her passion, values and inspiration with others.*

Tondra Devarel

Acknowledgements

Leigh Sistek
Certified Title Corporation
www.certifiedtitlecorp.com
Facebook: @leighmarianosistek
Instagram: Lms3502
LinkedIn: Leigh Mariano Sistek

It's Only a Chapter
Leslie Greene

"Our deepest fear is not that we are inadequate. Our deepest fear is that we are powerful beyond measure. It is our light, not our darkness that most frightens us... Your playing small doesn't serve the world. There's nothing enlightened about shrinking so other people won't feel insecure around you...As we let our own light shine, we unconsciously give others permission to do the same." Marianne Williamson

In 2012, I made it my mission to spread hope. I realize, in hindsight, that spreading hope meant so much to me then because I had lost all hope. Hopeless is an incredibly dangerous and lonely place to be. I never want anyone to feel as lost as I felt at that time. So like with many good missions, I set out to help others, unaware that I needed the help I so desperately wanted to give. It would take another year for my life to become a full-on Lifetime movie.

Leslie Greene

Our relationship started out as an incredible love story. I met this guy at a bar in Bethesda, MD. I was with a friend at her work party down the street. After the work party was over, everyone walked over to the bar. I had been intentional about thanking veterans for my freedom, so when we ran into some Marines, I noticed this one guy had clearly lost his eyes for my freedom. I broke off from my friend, walked up to him and thanked him for his service. We started talking. He was a good-looking guy; he just didn't have eyes. This didn't phase me at all. I wasn't flirting with him, because there was no pressure. I was just simply thanking a guy for my freedom. However, I did get his phone number to keep in touch. My goal was to offer support to the blinded Marine from someone who didn't even know him. I would have loved to have been supported for just being alive and I hadn't been through anything remotely as traumatic as what he had been through.

It was a week after the fun trip with my friend to Bethesda when I had a bat mitzvah to attend. One of the first prayers we read in the service was about seeing God. Not physically seeing God, but emotionally/spiritually seeing God. The prayer was beautiful. It made me think of the Marine with no eyes who couldn't see physically but surely could see spiritually. I held on to that prayer for the length of my

It's Only a Chapter

marriage to this guy. It's long gone now. But when I read the prayer a week after I met the Marine who sacrificed so much for my freedom, I thought of him. I saw it as a sign from God (I don't see signs from God that way anymore). I picked up the phone and called the blind Marine I had met the weekend before. We talked for two hours and it was great.

Two months later I drove to meet him in Alexandria, Virginia, about two hours north from where I lived. We started dating. I soon found out that he was filming an HBO documentary on surviving getting blown up in Iraq. James Gandolfini was the interviewer. "Did you want to come up to DC and attend the HBO documentary release party?" he'd asked. "Sure, that sounds great," I responded. It was very cool seeing the lights, famous actors, authors and more. It was dreamy in the beginning. It was also tough because I saw pictures of his broken body in the hospital for the first time and a film of blown up Humvees and war. I felt so blessed that this guy that I liked was alive. It created some draw toward him that I cannot explain, other than saying that is when our darkness started really being attracted to each other.

My then husband was receiving his first service dog and I got to fly down to Florida with him to meet her for the first time. I met her puppy raisers who had spent nine months raising her before they met. It was magical. My heart was so excited to be a part of this inspirational moment. I was a single mom with a great family and a great job. I just didn't have the money to be flying from state to state, needing ball gowns for this and that. But this guy had the money to support having me on his arm. I paint this picture for you because it truly was magical the first few months and I really got drawn in. I wanted my prayers to be answered.

Admittedly, we definitely drank too much alcohol and he lied to me about smoking pot - but isn't that the norm for people in their early 30's in a new relationship? It was my norm. About five months into the relationship, I had most of his passwords for his email, bank accounts, and other personal information. Our situation was different from two perfectly able people. He was a blind guy and I was looking to be saved from trying to make life work alone as a single mom. He asked for help with managing some life tasks and I was happy to help.

Things took a turn around six months in when I found the Craigslist communication where he was soliciting company. I lost it. He wasn't only lying about smoking pot, he was lying about another girlfriend and hooking up with strangers from Craigslist and God knows where else. But by then, I felt stuck. I was six months into this relationship and my son had met him, my family had met him, and I felt an attachment to him that I couldn't let go of. I was weak. I was living in fear of doing life alone. It's why I stayed with him after he cheated on me months into the relationship.

I had my first panic attack when we were going to an inaugural ball in 2008. I was in our bathroom in northern VA in a gorgeous royal blue satin ball gown, breathing into a paper bag, crying, trying to get back my breath. All major highways were shut down around Washington, DC for the inauguration. We were going to the VFW Ball. Biden was supposed to show up, but he didn't. There are a lot of inaugural balls. I was so anxiety ridden. I told him to go with his mom and stepdad who were on their way and that I didn't want to go. It blew his mind that I didn't want to go to an inaugural ball in Washington, DC. My anxiety was very new then. I really didn't know what this feeling was, but it freaked me out that the roads were closed. I was with a blind guy and his wonderful dog. I was responsible for them. A packed capital city with people in a closed space was the last place I wanted to be. There were people everywhere. This was just the beginning of my true quest to disappear.

Leslie Greene

In 2009, we were at my dad's military retirement in Florida when my then husband had a massive breakdown. We were in the parking lot of our hotel before my dad's retirement ceremony and we started yelling at each other about something and he began banging his head on our vehicle. He would bang his head on walls when he got really overwhelmed and frustrated. I have since learned that people banging their heads on walls is more common than I ever knew. To this moment I can remember crying so hard and not being able to breathe, somehow faking it through event after event. I don't remember how we got it together to show up for a ceremony for my dad that day. Disguising the disease had just become the norm.

The verbal abuse was demoralizing and usually went like "you have nothing, all the money is mine." The lies and the comments that left me feeling lonely and isolated were becoming everyday occurrences. After a year or so together, I quit my job and we moved to his hometown where his family was, four states away from mine. I didn't have to work. I didn't realize it at the time, but moving away from my family and not having my own income was isolating. I drove him to speaking engagements, and pretty much everywhere else he needed to go, and volunteered with many military organizations. It sounds cool until you realize

It's Only a Chapter

you have screwed yourself out of independence and can't see a way out because "you have nothing." I already felt like I was nothing before I met him and this was just becoming more of the nothingness I felt in myself. My shame for simply existing in the world.

We had been together for five years and were disagreeing for majority of that time before the last night we spent together. The tension had really been building for many months. I had been recording our conversations on my cell phone for fear of what was going to happen. One night he put his hands on me for the first and only time. I have no memory of him "moving me". I just had the black hand-shaped bruises on my arms to show where he moved me out of the way so that he could get to the loaded pistol in the safe. He had never threatened physical violence on me before and I don't believe he consciously chose to hurt me physically then either. We had spent years arguing leading up to this moment. He ended up holding a loaded pistol to his chest begging me to pull the trigger. Thankfully the loaded pistol wasn't pointed at me, but I would never. I don't remember anything between trying to stop him from getting to the safe in the back room and when he was holding the pistol to his chest in our bedroom. Eventually, I was able to get the gun and put it on the nightstand.

Leslie Greene

My son was about 16 years old then and came home shortly after the gun incident. I had put on a baseball cap and had been crying for hours. I was talking to my son in the bathroom because he had been sick when my then husband came in the bathroom and picked a fight with my son. He said something to him like, "you are not the king of this house, I am!" He was taking the fight outside, literally. When he walked out the front door thinking my son was going to follow, I had my son call 911. My son didn't know why I was telling him to dial 911; he hadn't been there for the gun part, and my ex-husband displayed unstable behavior often enough that my son was surprised he had to call 911. But he dialed and the police came.

The police separate two people in a domestic violence situation. I was outside and my ex-husband was inside with my son. It complicated the situation even more that my ex was a hometown hero. He beat the bomb. He came back home alive. Amazing, I agree. The officer that was inside with my ex and my son came out onto the porch where I was and said "there's nothing to worry about here. I've seen him on TV." All hope drained from my body. *There's nothing to worry about here?* Smoke and mirrors had been the life I lived in for years at this point. My life was an example of cognitive dissonance: a contradiction of beliefs and decisions to the way one acts and the way one wants to act. The mind f@$% that ensued was a treacherous path.

The officer with me had heard the whole story about the pistol being involved. The officer with my ex didn't hear anything about the loaded pistol. They ended up using the Baker Act on my husband. The Baker Act can be used by law enforcement, doctors, mental health professionals, and judges when someone is showing suicidal signs and extreme signs of violence. He was taken to the VA hospital on a 24-hour hold. The doctor called me the next day and told me he was doing better and should be able to come home. "What?" I asked, "Is that the typical hold time when a loaded pistol was involved in a domestic situation?" The doctor hadn't been told anything about the pistol. They kept him for 72 hours. Maybe it's like a game of telephone between the parties involved in trying to help. I told the police about the gun; they may or may not have told the VA. The doctor who saw my husband at the time didn't know and was about to send a very dangerous and broken man back to his family. Frightening.

It was truly shocking that no one in my husband's family was treating the situation as dire as my family was. I was advised not to be in the house when he returned from the VA hold. Thankfully, he ended up staying with his parents. He would come to our house while my son and I were out and pick up things and clean up, like make the bed and stuff. He didn't understand that he needed to stay away for a while. I ended up changing the locks on the house and he decided that we were getting divorced. At least he couldn't drive to the house or follow me around town without someone sighted being with him. It would have been a different situation for sure if he'd been sighted.

I've tried not to demean myself for not making the decision to leave with my son and letting my ex-husband be the one to decide it was over. Part of me would have loved to be the kind of woman who stood up for herself and knew where to draw the line. But I didn't. Part of me has tried to be invisible all of my life. Another part desperately wanted to be seen. I would get emotional every time someone thanked me for being with my ex; they saw me. Most people just talked to him and barely noticed me. I was safe. I felt sorry for anyone who had to see me: the 7-Eleven attendant, the stranger on the street. I thought "how sad for them that they had to see me."

I had decided to stay with a man with no eyes after he cheated, lied, and did worse to me because he could never see me. What a relief. And when I walked through the world with a good looking guy with no eyes, a beautiful guide dog, no one else saw me either. This was a very "safe" place for fearful me. I had become as invisible as I'd always dreamed of. Hopeless is an incredibly dangerous and lonely place to be.

By the time the divorce hearing rolled around a year later, I was in VA and he was still in FL. He told me not to worry about not being at the hearing, that he would take care of it. I called the court and they allowed me to dial in to the hearing. I cannot express how powerful it felt to be able to have my voice in that hearing.

Leslie Greene

For nine months after this incident, I did a 200-hour yoga teacher training. Every other weekend for nine months, I healed, learned, meditated, and cried my way through the trauma. Now I am a holistic health coach on a mission to spread hope to anyone who will listen. For me, peace and health is not natural. Oh, but how I yearn for it! It always seemed out of reach. But not anymore. Speaking my truth and releasing shame is the most freeing and spiritual thing I have ever done.

While driving out of town to move back home in 2014, I thought to myself "I have a story no one wants to hear." But I knew that someday I would have to tell the story for my own healing and for anyone who needed to hear it. People want to hear that the guy who beat the bomb and the nice girl made it. This was not the case. I lived so much of my life before and during that relationship in fear, not knowing that the pushing down of my true self and the shame I had was creating the bad stuff in my life. For a long time, I would give almost anything to keep this story quiet, but that's not the point of the chapter or the point of living honestly. The point of this chapter is to set free the chokehold of fear and exposure of being seen.

Just like this chapter, this time in my life was just part of my bigger picture. I never wanted this time in my life to be my story. It's just a chapter in the wonderful life of me.

Leslie Greene *is the founder of Leslie Greene Health Coaching and is an executive assistant at an investment bank. In 2012, Leslie declared it her mission to spread hope. With 25+ years in the health and wellness industry, Leslie is committed to advocating for health and coaching people through their wellness journey. Leslie has been a*

Leslie Greene

certified yoga instructor for over eight years and recently obtained her Institute for Integrative Nutrition Holistic Health Coach Certification. In addition, Leslie is certified in Mindful Yoga Therapy for Trauma.

Broken Pieces
Skyy Harrison

Psalm 23

The Lord is my shepherd; I shall not want. He makes me lie down in green pastures: He leads me beside the still waters. He restores my soul: He leads me in the paths of righteousness for His name's sake. Yes, though I walk through the valley of the shadow of death, I will fear no evil; for You are with me; Your rod and Your staff, they comfort me. You prepare a table before me in the presence of my enemies; You anoint my head with oil; My cup runs over. Surely goodness and mercy shall follow me all the days of my life; And I will dwell in the house of the Lord Forever. – New King James Version

Growing up, I always thought I had life all figured out. I just knew I would meet that perfect guy, get married and have one boy and one girl and live happily ever after. The end. If only things happened that way. I'm going to take you back to 2007. When finishing high school, I did not think I would meet a man who I thought was completely perfect. God's gift to women, at least that is how I felt in the beginning. One day I was giggling with my home girl, Dria, and just asked her playfully if she had a friend for me. She grinned and replied, "I do have someone for you. He is my boo's best friend." I had been in a funk and agreed to go with her that upcoming Saturday to meet him. All day that Friday I sat anxiously and nervously anticipating meeting who she spoke of. It turned out to be a weekend I will never forget.

Saturday night finally arrived and I was so excited to meet this guy. I remember pulling up at his mom's house as I sat on the passenger side of the car with my partner in crime. I cannot even explain how many butterflies were flying around in my stomach at that time. When we stepped out of the car, Dria introduced me to this tall, slender man who made me feel short as I had to look up to him and I'm 5'7 myself. He had long braids down his back, was light brown skinned, freckles (only noticeable if you were close enough), a chain around his neck, and light brown big eyes staring back at me. Just like that, an instant connection. Have you ever just felt like you've known someone forever although the two of you have never previously met? That was one of those moments where I felt like the universe was pulling two people back together who may have known each other in another lifetime.

After talking for what seemed like days, we all agreed to follow him home to his cottage in the woods as I used to call it. Dria's boyfriend, Dria and I, plus a friend of the family, all arrived at his house. Simply good times and good energy just continued on that whole night. When I say we laid there and talked and talked and talked, it felt like I was talking to my best friend. We fell asleep and he held me tight but was the perfect gentleman. All I could see was that man. From that day forward, I belonged to him before I even knew it. Days turned into months and we spent an increasing amount of time together. Everywhere he went, I went. He would call while passing through in his work truck to say, "I'm picking you up. You're coming with me." I would just light up eye to eye. For the first time in a long time I was so happy for what I thought was a man who had me in every way.

Things were fine for the first six months. When I say that man invested so much time in me. Not to mention, my one-year-old daughter absolutely adored him. One night turned into me moving in about a month later. I was so wrapped up in the love part that I did not notice what was going on right in front of my eyes. This man had me in my rarest form. I went from being in a dream relationship to wondering where I went wrong in a matter of moments. I went from being a stay-at-home spouse to victim very quickly. I used to clean, cook, care for the kids, have his towel and washcloth laid out before his shower and his clothes out after. It didn't matter what time he got home, I always got up and made that man's plate because I honestly thought he was working hard to support our family.

At first, I didn't even notice the change in his behavior. Was I that naive or was I truly that in love? Then somehow, the man I once could not find myself even a foot apart from was suddenly always away. I remember doing the laundry and finding things in his pockets that confirmed he was cheating. When I confronted him, he just denied it. I looked at him with pure utter disbelief, but of course, told him I believed him. Even though I had the proof, I allowed myself to believe his lie, because I wanted what he said to be the truth.

One day, while waiting for him to arrive home, I began thinking: *He won't let me work. He won't let me have a phone. He won't let me have a car.* I paced the floor back and forth in an effort to figure out how I could convince this man I needed a phone. He finally pulled around the back of the house. I stood at the glass door waiting to let him in. He barely made it through the door before I blurted, "with you being gone so much, I need a phone. What if something happens to one of the kids while you are away at work?" He then made sure I had a phone. Finally, I had a connection to the outside world! It was sad at one point. I remember having to hide a spare phone because I never knew if he would take mine. I made it back to the Myspace (a social network) world. I created a profile, and just like that, different women and their stories about this man - my man - just all started to hit me at once. For the first time, I figured out that the seclusion was not because he loved me and just wanted me to raise the kids and be home, but it was a play in his covering up his path plan. He wanted to make sure that I would never find out what he was doing.

That day, I waited for him to get home to confront him with this information. He finally arrived, and as normal, his things were out for his shower. I began to warm his plate as I heard the faucets turn off. I handed him his meal as I sat on the bed to continue watching Lifetime, which had become my best friend at this point in time. Finally breaking the silence, I asked, "So how long did you think this would continue before the truth came out?" He looked at me in confusion. I replied, "Yes, all your women have been in contact with me. And when I say all, it's more than I can count on my hands at a time." He retorted, "They're lying. Those girls just want your spot. Go ahead and be dumb and give it up over lies." So I retorted, "I am not so sure about the lies." Before I could utter the words out of my mouth that I was leaving and moving on, I was pounding on the bed with two hands around my neck. I was swinging and panicking, doing everything to release the grasp of this man's hands from around my throat. The aftermath was even worse. Blood vessels had popped in my eyes and it was like looking into the eyes of death. Bloody red was all anyone could see. For the first time, I feared this man. As the months went on of arguing and fighting, fighting and arguing, it seemed never-ending. Some days were good and others were really bad. I moved multiple times over the next three years and we were already in year five of dating at this time. The more days that went by, the harder it became. I loved that man, in spite of the trauma, and this I did not understand.

To the public, life was perfect. Everyone thought I had it made, but if they only knew the lifestyle I was truly living behind closed doors. I was a prisoner in my own home. It's crazy how my dream so quickly became a nightmare. On several occasions, I would have a bloody nose or lips. Anytime I mentioned me leaving it would become a bigger brawl. I remember our just months old beautiful baby girl at that time had become extremely ill out of the blue. Her neck had swollen up and her temperature was 108.4 and would not come down. The longer we stayed home, the sicker she got. He finally showed up and we rushed her to the hospital. The medical staff could not get her temperature down. She was rushed to MCV Hospital dead in the middle of winter with no clothes on because they were scared it would raise her temperature even more. When it was time to go to the hospital, I thought he was about to get in the ambulance with us. Instead, he said he and his cousin would stay home to let me know if there were any updates. In sheer disbelief, I laughed and jumped in the ambulance and we took off. For days, I slept at MCV with our daughter and to this day, no one can tell me what was wrong with her. When our daughter was finally discharged, we were headed home and he said something slick out the mouth. A fight broke out between us in the car on the way home. I was there; I was at my breaking point. He had endangered our daughter and didn't even care. I got home and intuitively knew someone had been in my house. Sometimes a woman's intuition is worse than a person's lie. We do not know how we know, but we do. Instantly, I knew my things had been moved. I'm a particular person, so everything of mine is always in place. To know that our daughter was lying in the hospital dying and he had the nerve to have a woman in my house, in my shower, and in our bed. I was livid and told him this could no longer be my home.

A couple more years passed and the abuse just became worse and worse. It was almost a part of our daily routine. The years continued to roll by and the more I left, the more he brought me back. I remember thinking one day that if I went to his parents, my issues would be over. The caliber of parents and grandparents they were, one could have never imagined that he could act in the manner he did. I was leaving and before I could make it across the yard, bam, my head hit the ground. He was on top of me, choking me, and not even caring that his parents were only feet away inside the house. His father came out immediately and removed him from off of me. Just like that, I was gone again. Then back again.

We were on about house number five at this point. He always moved us into better. I always had the best, but those material possessions were costing me the little bit of life left in me. I was pregnant now with our last child, our first boy. I thought finally having a boy would make him want to be a better person for him. His actions changed for a while but were soon right back to how they were before. I remember a time when my dad and mom showed up unexpectedly. He was gone of course. When I saw my dad getting out of the car with a shotgun, I just sat in silence. They hadn't known yet that he wasn't home. They asked me if he was putting his hands on me and I said "no, where did you all get that?" They said "it doesn't matter. As long as you are ok." Then they left. If they only knew the lie I told.

Weeks later, another argument began. Another woman was in the mix. That argument led to me being dragged through the whole house, outside off the balcony, down the stairs, through the car and back inside. When I found a little piece of strength, I managed to crawl to the couch. The next day I went into labor. I dared not mention to the doctor how this happened at eight months, but it was not my first rodeo. I had my son and he was indeed healthy and perfect. After arriving home and getting settled in with the new baby, everything was good for a while. I saw a major change in his behavior and attentiveness to our children and me. Of course, it was short-lived before the abuse started again. I was being kicked and spat on. For some reason, I was shocked. But I was to the point where I realized this was not love.

One day while sitting on the couch, a girl called who was mad at him because she caught him with another woman. As I sat there listening to her speak, I'm thinking the nerve of her calling his fiancé speaking of catching him with another woman, but she was just as guilty as the other girl. I called one of his friends and demanded he take me to the hotel the girl said he was at. He agreed as long as I didn't tell him. Indeed, his truck sat parked at this hotel. I stood outside and screamed "I know you're here. Come out! Come out nowwwww!" Since he refused to come out, I proceeded to the one thing he loved the most, his truck. Appearing like a ghost, there he stood. I said, "The nerve of you. I now see for myself. We are done. I will never come back." I jetted off, jumped in the car, went back home, and packed all of my and my children's things. By the time he decided to come back home, I was already gone! Gone - not a pack of noodles left in sight. I took it all but the furniture and never looked back. This was my final straw.

I had gotten away from this man who had almost a ten-year hold on me. I left with permanent scars but with life left in me. I began to start what I thought was a new life. I was living in my own house, driving the car he bought me at some point after leaving, was working a job, and had a dependable babysitter. I needed nothing from him. After time went by, we talked on and off and dated for a bit. He stayed with me for a while and vice versa. One day I was sitting in the living room and whoosh, my front door swung open and he walked in. Before I could run, he had already grabbed me by the bar stool at my kitchen table and dragged me across the floor next to the couch where my friend was sitting. He pulled out a gun and placed it under my chin. He looked me in my eyes and said, "You just got back from being with a man. I will kill you Skyy. Do you know that?" I stayed calm as Dria ran out the door screaming for help from my proprietor who lived next to me. She ran back in and said, "Stop D, this is not the way to go. Let her go." In an instant, something snapped back in him, and he came to and took off out the door. That was the scariest moment of my life, but looking back, I survived! The authorities took him to jail when they caught him. Day in and day out, I waited to hear from him. Can you believe it? Me…Skyy…wanted to hear from a man that could have taken my life. All I knew was I loved him, and he was the father of my children, and I did not want him in jail for ten years or more. The district attorney kept threatening me to testify and I refused. We were engaged at this point. I was like, this is it, finally he is changing to the point he gets it. Court came and I did not testify. After months of him being in jail, he was finally free! Our engagement went on for months, but the women never stopped.

Skyy Harrison

One day I just finally realized I deserved better. We went in separate directions and I kept communication limited and only about the children. He moved on and as did I and just like that, all the years wasted. But Psalm 23 mostly got me through on those hard days. I could hear my grandma reciting it repeatedly in my head. Not only was I finally standing on my own two feet, but I, Skyy Harrison, had survived abuse.

***Skyy L. Harrison** is a phenomenal mother of ten. After pushing through all struggles and overcoming so many obstacles in life, she's continually motivated to want more and do more! She's currently pushing to finish school to become an RN, which inspired her to pursue entrepreneurship with the launch of her* *nurses and doctors scrub line. Focused, motivated and ambitious all describe this supermom. With over 11 years in the customer service and retail industries, she is consistently building and expanding on connections. In her free time, she loves being involved in her community and consistently seeks out opportunities for continued personal and professional development.*

Skyy Harrison

Acknowledgements

Lisa Bostic
Bostic Suites LLC
Email: Stl21@bosticsuitesllc.com
Facebook: @bosticsuitesllc

Julie Hill
The WOW Collaborative
thewowcollaborative.com

Janene Bridgeforth
Forever Memories LLC
www.forevermemoriesllc.com
Facebook: Forever Memories
Instagram: @Forever_Memories_320

Irvin Scott
Tip's Hang-Em high
Facebook @Irvinscott
Instagram: @tip37toe

The Raw Truth or a Dirty Lie
LaKesha Monroe

Galatians 5:1: "It is for freedom that Christ has set us free. Stand firm, then, and do not let yourselves be burdened again by a yoke of slavery."

Life has shown me just how strong I am. Growing up, I always wanted to be the next Florence Griffith Joyner. I loved running but, as my life changed, I found myself running away from myself. Let me explain. I grew up in a home that was full of life then it later turned into darkness. My abusive home showed me how to put on two faces. The first face was on when I had to fight off my mom's boyfriend while molesting me and being scared to tell my mother because I didn't want to be the person who ruined her happiness. He would give me money all the time and it was probably to silence me, but I didn't think about it at the time. I would spend it on friends. The other was the angry face where people thought I looked mean just because I wanted to, when the whole time, I was fighting against suicide because not telling my mom about the sexual abuse was tearing me up inside. I really wanted to tell someone, but didn't out of fear of becoming the talk of the town. Once I finally told my dad, I regretted not telling him sooner because when I did, I could tell it broke his heart to know I had been violated.

Even though our home had great times, things changed when my mom's relationship changed. After surviving childhood abuse, I then became a teenage mother. Older men constantly attempted to pursue me. One day while hanging with a friend, a guy placed a gun to my head because he didn't believe I was a teenage mother. He thought I was at least 18, although it wasn't uncommon for teens to look a little older than they were. Once he removed that gun from my head I ran home crying. My mother was asleep so I didn't wake her or my brother. I just bottled it up inside and thanked that good friend for saving my life. If she hadn't been there that night, that man probably would've raped me. A few months later, he was killed and since he died, I felt no need to tell my parents because he wouldn't harm me again. However, I still was fighting the traumatizing secret of potentially being raped or murdered that night.

As the years passed, I continued to bury the feelings of being violated and never asked myself, "why me?" I just wanted to live a normal life that included work, family, hanging with my friends and taking care of my son. I worked to shift my focus from self-love to mental survival. Being a person who loves to help people, I poured my love into others to avoid dealing with the real problem: ME. Mental abuse was just as bad for me as sexual and physical abuse. Once my mind was in a place of hate about myself, it allowed me to let go of myself. I began eating to avoid dealing with my problems. Those problems led me to an abusive relationship that lasted over three years. I was waking up to hits across the face, arguments before work and coming home from work fighting until sunrise. He would say, "Come on, bring that man out of you." Somehow I thought that was love because I didn't love myself enough to know it wasn't healthy. I used to say, "There is no way I could let a man abuse me after seeing my mom go through it." Then here I was in a similar situation and too afraid to walk away. Especially after that night. That dark night near those railroad tracks when another gun was placed to my head telling me he would kill me. I closed my eyes praying for peace and hoping God would save me. Suddenly, my boyfriend placed the gun back in his pocket and I dropped him off at home. I didn't cry because my nerves were really fucked up. I didn't even sleep that night. I just wondered how the hell I got into this shit. The next morning, I got a voicemail: "Kesha, wake up girl!" I woke up and went and picked him up. I stayed with him at his cousin's house. He apologized, then said "That's why you don't fuck with me. You know I love you and nobody else wants you but me."

I realized over time that because my mentality was fucked up, I really did accept all his shit and thought it was love. I was so stupid and I couldn't believe all the shit I put up with. I didn't need him. He needed me. I let him drive my car while I went to work, among other things, and he constantly took advantage of me. One night I cooked for him and thought about poisoning him but thought, "Naw, I can't leave my mom and aunt to raise my son. They've already done so much." Because I knew he was crazy, I wanted to protect my family so I just stayed with him. That is, until I really got tired. One day I just left and stopped answering his calls. I had finally gotten the strength and courage to physically leave, but mentally I was still connected to his words: "No one will want you but me." He moved on to another woman but I would still visit his family because his sister and I were close. One day we were at a card game and he began to talk shit about my family. I couldn't take it anymore. I flipped the table over and began choking him until he couldn't breathe. I knew he had asthma, but in that moment I was done with the mental and physical abuse I'd taken. When his family broke up the fight, he got one good slap to my face. I grabbed a knife that was on the counter but his sister snatched it from me. That was the last time my ex ever tried to fight me.

I asked myself all the time "how did I allow mental abuse to take over me?" I really needed some guidance and support. My dad lived near me but wasn't there the way I needed him to be. One day an angel spoke to me and suggested I seek counseling. I called a hotline and began working with a counselor. When we began my journey to healing, it opened some wounds and I knew something had to change in order for me to grow. I was tired. Tired of putting up two faces when I really wasn't ok. I fought to start loving myself again. My cousin, Angel, helped pull me out of a dark place. She helped me slowly get back to myself. For example, she knew I really didn't like earrings so we started searching for some cute hoops. Then we explored wigs. She knew I didn't always hate myself, so she helped me to see what she saw - my beauty and strength that still existed while surviving mental, sexual and physical abuse.

Everything begins in the mind. When I began to change my thoughts, I wanted to change everything else in my life for the better. I wanted to GROW and be more than the evil bitch people thought I was and start loving me more. Counseling, praying and journaling brought me closer to God. I prayed for forgiveness over my abusers and forgiveness for not telling my parents what I experienced. I sought forgiveness for not allowing them to protect me and being scared they wouldn't believe me. I didn't want to be judged because mentally, I don't believe I could've handled it.

As I continue to heal, I've learned that it's okay to not be okay.
- It's okay to say NO to protect your PEACE.
- It's okay to have bad days, just don't stay there.
- Don't hold things inside; have the difficult conversations.
- SELF-LOVE is LOVING YOURSELF TO THE FULLEST THROUGH ALL YOUR MISTAKES.
- GROWTH IS NECESSARY BECAUSE OTHERWISE YOU DIE LIVING IN THE PAST.

Not being honest with yourself is the dirty lie that stays covered up. When you live in your raw truth, you become free. The wind really feels like a breath of fresh air. Now when I smile, I am genuinely happy and when I'm sad, I know that it's okay as long as I'm not there for too long. I'm still healing but I am far from where I used to be. Having more FAITH in GOD was the start. God began to place the right people in my life which is how I'm able to tell this story of being PERFECTLY IMPERFECT. Admittedly, I'm still removing some layers to be completely free of my past. Counseling is great therapy because I've learned that speaking with a stranger who offers no judgement has allowed me to show more emotions that I have never expressed. I feel good after speaking with my therapist because I always end our sessions with a clearer understanding of who I am. The tears mean I am releasing and the smiles mean I am evolving into the person I am meant to BE. My story is already written. I just have to follow God's plan to live out my purpose.

The Raw Truth or a Dirty Lie

LaKesha Monroe is the CEO of TwentyFourVii Candle Co. As a domestic violence survivor, she often volunteers her time to the Carol Adams Foundation and TheFacesBehindAPurposeForYou for other victims of domestic abuse. She is a proud caregiver to her mother and her autistic son.

LaKesha Monroe

Acknowledgements

Sonya Washington

Jamita Taylor

Candice Turner
Facebook: Candice Turner
Instagram: @howaboutac
LinkedIn: Candice N. Turner

Daphney Robinson

Stay Woke
Jameka Smith

I thought it was a dream until I had been physically woken by the loud banging noise coming from the back door. I jumped up, startled, but headed to the door, and peeped through the peephole. To my surprise, it was him, "Tony". I walked away from the door thinking to myself, *why is he here*? I thought I made it clear that I wanted nothing else to do with him.

It was all good just a week ago.

I was in the club having the time of my life. Every song was my song. Couldn't tell me I didn't look good. Couldn't tell me I didn't have rhythm. My friend Dutchess had called earlier that day asking if I was still attending what was labeled the hottest birthday bash of the year. I had been home from an incarceration of three years for eight months now, so yeah, I felt the need to step on scene. I had purchased a cute fitted sweater and leggings, that were a size smaller to be sure they fit every curve I owned, plus a pair of thigh high boots that complimented my thighs so nicely. Oh, you couldn't tell me nothing!

In my mind, I didn't feel the need to invite my fiancé, Tony, along to the party, because that wasn't his scene. Tony didn't like to party, at least that's what he told me. I met Tony a little over a year ago from a previous job I was working at while incarcerated. We clicked and had been kicking it ever since. Tony was my boo. I told Dutchess I'd meet her down bottom (what we call Shockoe Bottom in Richmond, VA) around 10:00. I decided to drive so that when I was ready to dip, I could. The party was jumping, the music was lit, and it was a nice crowd. The energy in the room was as if I'd never left. I guess it's safe to say your girl still had it. Heads were turning left and right. A vibration started coming from my purse. It was an alert on my phone I'd never seen before saying "Find my iPhone". I placed my phone back in my purse and continued to the bar to grab a drink to loosen up a little more. I was tense and I had no idea why. Before I could leave the bar, my phone did a thing again. This time Dutchess was there to witness this alert.

"Jay, I'd been calling you to tell you to grab me a drink while at the bar, but your phone is off," she said. Puzzled, "my phone can't be off. Tony just paid our bill," I replied. Dutchess said, "I called three times. It's off Jay." I looked down at the phone again and there was that same alert, "FIND MY IPHONE". This was getting annoying, but it had to be a malfunction, because clearly my phone was in my hand. I refused to let this be a distraction from the party. It was turnt in there and it was time I turned up.

Dutchess and I returned back to the VIP section sipping, dancing and vibing. I was having fun and the night was still young. I wasn't ready to go home. A couple of others that had been partying with us that night suggested an after-hours spot. Shit, I was down, so after hours it was. It was on the southside of Richmond, VA where I was from, born and raised. Dutchess said, "Jay, your car is good in the club's parking lot. Leave it there and ride with us." Bet! As we approached the 804 Lounge, my phone did a thing again: "FIND MY IPHONE". This time I turned it off, which became my worst mistake.

804 Lounge was jumping, more than the club we'd just left. People were wall to wall and I

headed to the bar line. It wasn't a crowd I wanted to be around, so I sipped fast, danced a little, and before I knew it, it was 5:00 in the morning. I'd had enough. I was ready to go, but then I was reminded that I didn't drive. I tried to text Dutchess, and to my surprise, my phone really was off. I needed answers as to why. The ride back to my car was quiet. My mind was racing and I had that feeling again of worry, nervousness. I was tense and, for the life of me, I didn't know why. I said my goodbyes and proceeded to head home. Completely unaware that I was being followed home, I pulled into the back alley of the crib. I began to tremble, but I'm thinking it's the liquor. Then from the side of my eye, I saw headlights. *Who could this be at this hour?* I thought. *And why are they sitting behind my truck?* Alarmed, I left the headlights on. Before I could react, the driver side door opened and it was Tony, my fiancé. Tony seemed different. He was angry, and before I could say anything, he said, "look at you bitch, all drunk and dressed like a slut. Hope you had fun. Let's ride."

"What's your issue with me Tony?" I asked. He said, "nothing" in response. I said, "I went out with some friends. Why I gotta be all that?" He then grabbed my arm roughly and snatched me out of the truck. I stumbled. Yes, I was intoxicated. I'd had several drinks during the course of the night and they were definitely kicking in. I was afraid, so I jerked away from him. He then grabbed me by the neck, and in doing so, scratched some skin off in the process, and it was visible. He said it again, "let's ride."

I heard "get your hands off my fucking daughter." It was my mom. I know that voice from anywhere. Thank You, God! I thought to myself. While he was distracted, I ran off to the back door of my house. I got in, shut the door and fast. Tony was outside of the door yelling "if you don't come back outside, I'm calling the police and telling them you got drugs in the house." I replied, "Do what you gotta do but I'm not coming outside with you, Tony. You're scaring me. I'm not riding with you anywhere. Go home, Tony. You're doing too much. We'll talk tomorrow."

Moments later, there was a knock at the front door. It was, in fact, the police. "Hello ma'am. Are you Jameka Smith?" I responded, "Yes I am." The officer goes on to say he got a call that I have drugs in my house and a report of suspicious activity. I opened the door wider and saw Tony talking to another police officer on the sidewalk. I stepped out on the porch to speak with the officer to let him know there weren't any drugs in the house and this was clearly a domestic call. I showed him the visible scratches on my neck from where Tony had just assaulted me right before they arrived. The officer then observed the scratches, took pictures of my neck, and proceeded to ask what happened. While I'm explaining, Tony yells out, "She hit me first! I was defending myself." I continued to tell the officer my side of the story. I was then instructed by the police to take out a restraining order and to file a warrant against Tony for assault. The officers escorted me to the police station to do just that. My mother followed to make sure I was safe and to provide a ride back home for me. To my surprise upon entering the station, Tony is also there trying to file a warrant against me for a supposed assault. The magistrate denied the warrant and said, "Clearly you have no signs of assault sir. Ma'am, come with me." I filed the necessary paperwork for a restraining order and the assault then went home. I was so hurt and confused as to why Tony would behave this way. I thought he loved me. I felt bad that it had come to this. I loved this man, but who was this man, really? Did I really know? So many things ran through my mind that night. I barely slept. Between my thoughts and Tony blowing my phone up, I'd gotten no rest and it was now 10 am. I was beginning to regret even calling the phone company to have my service restored.

A few days had gone by. I had stayed occupied with work and the kids, which I felt was the best way to get past what had taken place. There was no way I would give Tony another chance. My mind was made up. I broke up with him and there would be no reconciliation. He wasn't the man for me. My kids were affected by this, as well as my mother and stepfather. I deserved better and my kids deserved better. I began to get calls from private numbers and I knew it was him. I rejected the calls, so he tried calling from his work phone. I blocked that number too.

It had been over a week and I felt better about the situation. I was ok and my kids felt safe again.

What Doesn't Kill You Only Makes You Stronger!!!

My oldest and youngest were sick with an upper respiratory infection, so I kept them home from school today. We had fallen asleep in the living room.

Jameka Smith

I'm afraid to open the door. He's banging and yelling, "I just wanna talk to you. Open the door." I don't open the door and instead, ask him to leave. He yells out, "Open the fucking door or I'm gonna kick it in!" I yell "You're not supposed to be here. You're scaring my kids. Leave Tony, before I call the police." By now, my kids are awake from the noise and are hollering for me to come back in the living room with them. They're afraid. I go to grab my phone to call the police but before I can reach the living room, I hear glass breaking and lots of noise. It's the kitchen window. Unique, my daughter, screams "come on momma!" We all run out the front door - no shoes, no coat, no nothing. Not knowing where to go, we run into the corner store. It's lunch hour so the store is busy. I turn to the woman working behind the food counter and say, "Please hide my kids. Take them, please." She looks confused. Before I can explain what's happening, a voice says to me, "Come back to the house with me or I'm gonna kill you right in front of your kids." It's Tony talking while pulling a knife from a backpack in his hands.

As I look around the store, it's several men getting food on their lunch breaks, the cashier who was one of the store owners, and the woman who cooks the food. My kids and I were on our own, so I made a choice in order to keep my kids safe. He draws the knife on me and forces me out of the store. I make him drag me, stalling anyway that I can. I'm dragging my feet and he's grabbing my arm harder. I look behind me and all around me. Behind me is my next door neighbor. I can tell she heard the break-in and is aware of what is happening. She's on her phone and I'm praying she's talking to the police. She has fear and concern in her eyes. Shit, I would too if it were the other way around. She stays back but is near. The house is getting closer and closer. I dread what's going to happen next.

I'm tripping up the steps as he's forcing my steps. He's repeatedly saying, "If you not gonna be with me, you not gonna be with anybody." My mind is racing. What is really happening? "That's not true," I say to him. "I don't want anybody else. I want you. I love you." At this moment, I would tell him anything he wants to hear to change his mind. Clearly he's not in his right mind. He's got me at knife point. He pushes me inside, slinging me around, yelling, and being aggressive. He says, "Why haven't you been answering my calls or texts? You got me blocked. You don't wanna be with me. You're lying." He takes the knife and stabs me in the top of my shoulder. "Ahhhhhh!" I scream.

Shortly after, the paramedics arrived to take us both to the hospital. I didn't know his condition and I didn't care. He tried to kill my family and me. After several surgeries and 27 days later, I was reunited with my kids and family and it was the best feeling in the world. With rehabilitation, wound care, therapy, and lots of love, I made it, we made it. Unfortunately, Tony didn't make it. End of story.

Jameka Lynn Smith was born and raised in Richmond, VA and currently resides in Henrico, VA. She has three beautiful daughters, Miyanna, Maraia, and Kayla, and a grandson due in January

Stay Woke

2023. Jameka has been working since the age of 16 and is currently employed at a warehouse with Sauer Brands. Writing has always been one of her greatest hobbies and even as a child, she would carry a notebook and pencil with her everywhere she went to write down her thoughts. She has a degree in Human Services and is certified as a Personal Care Aide and Pharmacy Technician. Jameka has also done some work for FEMA as a Hazard Mitigation Counselor, counseling those affected by disasters in different states. In her spare time, she enjoys playing Bingo.

Jameka can be reached by email at jamekasmith35@gmail.com or on Facebook as Jameka Smith.

Acknowledgements

Shateeka Benjamin

Shenell Holmes
Kidzsequisite LLC
Facebook: @Shenellholmes
Instagram: @Kidzsesquiste

Remonia Cosby

Tina Gilliam
Facebook: Tina Gilliam

Teresa Terry
Teresa's Wigs
Facebook: Teresa's Wigs
Instagram: @teresaswigs

Jason Temple
BlessedBeauti Industries
Facebook: Temp Jay
Instagram: @iamtempjay

Shawnell Thompson
Thompson & Co. Home Improvements & More, LLC.
Facebook: Thompson & Co. Home Improvements & More, LLC.
Instagram: @Thompsonnco

Conclusion

Thank you for taking the time to read this book. It took a tremendous amount of strength and courage for these women to share their stories. The reality, however, is that their sharing was a selfless act. As you've read, these women were strong enough to break free from the stronghold of their abusers. In sharing their stories of survival, it is with great hope that they inspire someone else to be set free.

Life is a precious gift, given to us only once. It is intended to be lived fully, securely, safely, and happily. No one has the right to take that away from you. It is yours.

If you or someone you know is experiencing abuse, help is available. It may be difficult to find a way out, but there is a way out.

For a domestic violence or abuse situation, call the National Domestic Violence Hotline at **1-800-799-7233**. If you suspect child abuse or potential harm, call or text the Childhelp National Child Abuse Hotline at **1-800-422-4453**. For sexual assault support, call the RAINN National Sexual Assault Hotline at **1-800-656-4673**.

www.ingramcontent.com/pod-product-compliance
Lightning Source LLC
Chambersburg PA
CBHW051947160426
43198CB00013B/2335